Sleeping On Trains

Adriana Wood

Sleeping On Trains

Sleeping On Trains
ISBN 978 1 76041 290 6
Copyright © text Adriana Wood 2012, 2014
Cover photo: Adriana Wood
Author photo: Suzanne Rutherford

Poems in this collection were first published by Ginninderra Press in
Sleeping On Trains With Strangers (2012)
and *Sunset* (Pocket Poets 5, 2014)

This combined collection first published 2017 by
GINNINDERRA PRESS
PO Box 3461 Port Adelaide SA 5015
www.ginninderrapress.com.au

Contents

Sleeping On Trains With Strangers	7
Fish	8
Poem for Virginia Woolf	9
Poetry in Purple at the Markets	10
The Silence	11
A Ghost Story	12
Gypsies and Tinkers!	13
An Irish Immigrant's Hopes	14
The Funeral of Grace (or 'Another Bloody Funeral')	15
Circular Quay Sydney at Night	16
A Nightmare Holiday	17
Wolf	18
On Seeing Castles in Europe for the First Time	19
The girl and the ocean	20
Drifting	21
Australia and the Dreamtime	22
End of a Queensland Day	23
Bushfire	24
The Rainbow	25
After the Rain	26
A Different Beach	27
The Fortress	28
Nature's Alchemy	29
Pastel People	30
Memories of the Waikato, NZ	31
Bad Attempts at Haiku	32
Six-line Stories	33
Meanwhile, On the Other Side of Town…	34
Elvis Has Left the Building	36
Sunset	37

The Minotaur	38
Girl From Ithaca	39
Strawberries	40
Poetry Versus Commerce	41
Youth in their beauty	42
A Puppy From the Skies	43
Upon Gazing Into the Internet	44
Elegy for the many lone deceased women…	45
Travels to my spare room	46
Redundancy	47
For a friend	48
Susan	49
High On Tea	50
A Storyteller	51
The light of my words	52
Soulmate	53
Another Fake	54
Out Shopping	55
No More Stories and Poems	56

Sleeping On Trains With Strangers

A train glides beside the platform.
I join long carriages of somnambulant commuters.
We fly through forest and hills,
    while trees flash by like armies
        from the shadowy world of Tolkien.
In this wordless, silent, twilight world,
    strangers snatch extra sleep,
        dragged early from their beds.
I write poetry in a hard, upright seat.
Dictates of commerce bind me
    to this twilight-dawn world,
I must exchange coast, trees and poetry
    for city rituals of commerce,
        departing at dawn to return at dusk,
            sleeping on trains with strangers.

Fish

We set out, not to build a house, but to build strength in each other's lives.
We planned to birth love in each other.
But while I brought you gifts you sold them.
I thought you were a gentle Piscean, a fish.
You got yet another short-lived job in a fish shop.
I gave you spiritual gifts but you lost them.
Pisces means to be born by turquoise seas, in golden climes.
Pisces means to hate hate, love love, and scorn scorn.
Aquarius is to reason with reason, uphold truth for truth, and believe in belief.
Yet our fates are entwined in a battle to reconcile love and hate, while love seems weak and hate is strong.
Base instincts engulf soul desires,
    scorching us with fire.
Why do we get it so wrong?

Poem for Virginia Woolf

She was unique, ephemeral.
Now she is vanished, gone.
    from sight, sound and senses,
Her words no longer fly
    like bright birds from a cage,
    through her pen on the page.
The jigsaw puzzle of her ephemeral vision
    is broken and scattered,
        terminated early by death.
We live in the legacy of her sea of words
    that beat against the harsh, grey shores
        of a sterner, harsher reality.

Poetry in Purple at the Markets

Lyrical beneath the jacaranda trees, in full bloom,
    where a poetess recited, in purple, reflecting the blueish-mauve flowers,
    that listened to her words, spellbound.
Nearby children frolic'd in Dolphin Fountain,
    an ancient mosaic from Roman times,
    or so it seemed,
    scene and mosaics steeped in Roman, purple hues, and blue.
Delicate pavilions dotted the green, of stalls of artwork and
    treasures from a simpler age of handcrafts and simple pleasures.
Words lock the mind of creator, viewer and listener,
    speaking on, floating and hovering
    while the artwork spoke a different language.

The Silence

We mourn not because they are dead, their words no longer
    flying free as birds while they lie
        rigid, motionless, free now, through death, from fear of dying.
'They have departed to a better world,' it is said by mourners
    in the chapel as they are led,
        believing that now in heaven, the departed are happy,
where they have made their bed.
We do not mourn because their soul has departed to dimensions
    unseen in time and space,
        above a trench in the dank earth one cold September day,
            an abyss in heart and soul.
We mourn because their presence is felt no more.
Their voice, their laughter, the familiar footstep on the stair, no longer lingers.
No longer can we walk, talk, chat, email, and argue.
Our festive Christmas is replaced by eternal Easter.
We can no longer not speak to each other, after a quarrel.
This time the long silence is final.
They may have gone to glory, but silence
    renders a finite end to their earth story.

A Ghost Story

Every year, on the anniversary of his death, one bleak September, his wraith remembers…
And an unseen presence steals into my bed, while I lie in
    trancelike sleep.
I feel cold with horror, in the dark, feeling invisible caresses,
Unable to move or speak, in trancelike sleep.
Until light swirls through the curtains white mist, signalling
    morning,
I lie motionless, afraid the ghostly presence still lingers in my bed,
To be stirred by movement, if I awaken.
But the room is empty, serene, filled with white light, revealing I
    am alone.
The ghost has fled.
The wraith has flown back to the ethereal night where he dwells.
My night is his ethereal light, his light my night.

Gypsies and Tinkers!

My mother was an Irish immigrant, and for her children her dreams were bold.
She tells tales of her childhood, as an unloved orphan, to inspire me to get rich and lucky.
I learned the lesson wrong, I am told,
By working to help the poor and unlucky, which will not lead me to a leprechaun's pot of gold.
She wants my nose stuck up so high, I do not notice people floundering and falling down far below.
'You help Gypsies and tinkers!' my Irish aunt snorts, with angry frown.
'Gypsies and tinkers!'
My aunt disowns me, taking to her bed.
She implores my older sisters to write to her instead.
But towards the end of her life, I like to think my mother feels I am right,
Remembering she was once one of those forced into endless night.

An Irish Immigrant's Hopes

Molly was Irish born and orphaned young, made to work hard for roof and board.
Expected to be grateful at being saved from the streets, she was denied schooling.
Molly held a dream her future children would be free, in New Zealand, so she ran away to that free land, where education was denied to none.
In New Zealand, Molly proudly dressed her son for school in Sunday best, out of respect for the guardians of learning.
The other boys, mean in threadbare clothes, and bare feet, pounced on him in glee, dragging him around a football field, by his feet, proud at this cowardly feat.
Molly pondered, like many parents before and since,
'Why should learning be of the rule of the fist, and the laws of prejudice, and why are some schools like training camps for prison?'

The Funeral of Grace
(or 'Another Bloody Funeral')

We feel like professional mourners, as we stand around at the crematorium.
Grace, the deceased, did not know the preacher.
Clearly he did not know her, who did not believe in God.
His Rolf Harris face looks out of place, as he searches for saccharine words,
He exhorts us to be comforted by fond memories of Grace, whose army sergeant ways had not endeared her in the office.
I imagine Grace rising from her coffin, condemning the preacher's long hair and untidy beard, his saccharine speech about love and heaven.
'Rubbish,' she would loudly declare, but there is silence.
Lazarus does not arise.
A single trumpet sounds in tribute to Grace's war service.
We mutter hasty condolences, like a taped chorus, to her nephew.
'It was in her sleep,' we murmur. 'Painless – the best way to go.'
'She tippled a lot and took pills…bad for the heart,' he said ruefully, correcting our and the preacher's careless lies.
He hastily gathers his brood of unruly children, rushing off.
We stand round, eating stale cake, discussing who will die next,
    is death the end, and where do we go next.
'Another bloody funeral. Back to work,' a workmate declares,
    as we leave, Graceless.

Circular Quay Sydney at Night

A snake of lights curves along the shore.
Behind shells of the Opera House, the slick sea gleams like ebony, catching glistening light, in hard, sculpted waves.
Crowds of people spill out of cafes and bars.
Men and women are strident, restless, talking, laughing.
Sweat shines on skin in humid darkness while bare flesh is strobed by neon light.
Voices cry out as if to provoke a fight.
Laughter, shrill and tense, shrieking voices, form part of the cacophony of the street and traffic.
They are the harlequins of the night, who by the morning light vanish, no longer daring to lurk.
Replaced by brisk secretaries and businessmen,
Enveloped in harsh daylight by towering skyscrapers.
The day has taken back these denizens of the night.

A Nightmare Holiday

Only the whirring wings of flying things in the air, the empty sound of air.
No angels are near.
Only the hiss of waves that pitch and toss, in a formless rhythm, singing a rhyme unknown.
She is alone.
Only the sounds of voices that curse and swear,
The senseless babble of meaningless fools'
They try to touch and leer, speaking the meaningless language of fear.
Only the breath of fools fuelled by alcohol, drugs and hate.
To them she is only prey, now slipping away.
Eluding the man pack in the creaking maze, she glides like a fleeing shadow, through narrow corridors, up and down clanging metal gangways.
The cruise ship creaks and groans like a ghost ship, with curses, as the hunters fall back, grunting and puffing, finally losing footing in their hot pursuit.
She has gotten away.
The bright lady of the sea, the *Fair Star*, once a hospital ship for war-wounded, is haunted by groans of the sick and dying.
Added now are shadows and frantic breathing, desperate footfalls, of hunters, and their prey, one haunted, nightmare holiday.

Wolf

Wolf hunting in a pack, thriller,
    invader, hunter killer, slipping into
    peaceful pastures with your dark lean-ness.
Like a sliver of night,
    dark wedge in the sunlight, while
    raw, doleful keening interrupts the choirs of birds,
    fallen silent, in fear, songs strangled.
Wolf, you are like the shadows in dark suburban places.

On Seeing Castles in Europe for the First Time

Did gentle maidens sit beneath these castle window slits?
Weaving tapestries and dreaming of love?
Did knights bold mount these castle ramparts?
To defend them from foe,
Stealing out of the dark green woods?
These mighty castles, now only bastions of history and memories,
    endure, amidst trees, lakes, gardens, and bright peacocks,
    while tall skyscrapers blink their glassy windows
    high above the castle's walls.
Future meets past while destiny meets history.
Will these monuments to modern economy
    dominate the green expanses entirely?

The girl and the ocean

King Neptune, carried by white horses in the waves, spoke to
 a lone girl on the shore.
'Girl by the sea,' King Neptune called, 'Tell me your secrets of
the sea and how you strayed near my kingdom.'
'We could go together, you and I,
 to explore the seas within where secrets lie.
Mysterious secrets come to light, in dreams at darkest night.
Secrets that are veiled in daylight are revealed in moonlight.
Sad girl by the sea, talk to me, and tell me your secrets.
Join me beneath the green seductive seas,
 with the seaweed and the fishes,
 and broken-hearted wishes.'
She heard the sighing of murmuring oceans.
It was as if the sea was calling.
The surf seemed to stamp hooves and whinny, or was it the
scream of the gulls soaring above?
The pounding waters roared in her head.

Drifting

Sometimes I feel cut off, alone,
    drifting helplessly in an autistic society,
    driven by what society thinks I ought to do.
I feel like a wanna-be who feels like a never-been,
    going nowhere envious of has-beens,
Because they at least have been someone somewhere sometime.
People have so many cut and dried answers.
They give me the answers before I have even asked the questions.
I am made to feel as if I have no destiny,
    apart from a sad repetition of what happened yesterday.
Tomorrow I must find the key to unlock this prison,
    find out who I am, escape other people's expectations of me,
    TO BE FREE!

Australia and the Dreamtime

In Aboriginal lore the creator dreamed of Australia,
    so Australia came to be.
Spun on dreams, basking in the sun, washed by salty surf on parched shores, now spawning
    futuristic cities of skyscrapers.
Ancient Australia, sprawls like a giant reptile clinging to the matrix of the earth.
Bony backbone rearing towards the sky, Australia
    is also a land of gentle rolling hills, yellow grass,
    aromatic gum trees with grey-green leaves,
    pale skin, like the white man who called her home.
Meanwhile gum trees writhe in fantastic twisted shapes with
    souls of tribal dancers, proclaiming
    their oneness with the misty, undulating hills.

End of a Queensland Day

The twilight lingers over gum trees,
    slender, pale, in a mist of aromatic leaves.
Mist wraps itself around the slender trees like a trailing scarf.
The sky is like a curved bluish shell touched with pink.
The song of birds and cricket begin to die.
In Queensland the night moves quicker than a black panther.
The warm sounds of the day are hushed.
Darkness envelops all except for golden stars flickering above
    golden haze, in the vast canopy of sky.
It is the end of another Queensland day.

Bushfire

Bushfire sweeps burning,
Driven down slopes, twisting, turning.
A roaring inferno burns up sky and horizon further than eye can see, faster than car can travel, while explosions rip the air like missiles.
The bush has become like an army on fire.
Guided only by a fiery glow, at their backs, on the horizon, that is neither sun, moon nor god,
A young girl and her brothers march all night, seeking help.
Acrid smoke hangs in the air, in their breath, their eyes, their blistered lips and clothing black with grit.
In the harsh daylight, while the sun blazes like a bushfire overhead, ashes of parents and family house are exposed, burnt on memory like a negative on film.
Surviving trees are like twisted black characters on the page of the sky, writing about some ghastly war of nature's doing.
Arsonists may have lit the first match.
Families, and fearless bushfire volunteers, sights
    burnt in their hearts for many years to come, feel
    the guilt of survivors, mourning their dead.
Those the fire spares are the victors.

The Rainbow

Lantana, a despised weed, rambles wild, entangling the long grass in a vacant lot.
A purple flower dares to raise its head from the tangled leaves, growing its face towards a rainbow.
The rainbow, like an archway spanning the ocean, against stormy skies, shines like a blessing.

After the Rain

The rain has polished leaves, sky and rooftops, reflecting
    sunlight glistening through raindrops.
Yellow light drips through the trees, shining through
    raindrops suspended from grass and leaves.
The dusty, yellow earth, swirls like a serpent, greedily absorbing
the rain, which lies in dark streaks of moisture on the ground.
The trees are festooned with random raindrops, suspended like
crystals all around.
The bellbird's call pierces the silence in the dell,
    sweet and clear, like a Tibetan prayer bell.

A Different Beach

On Bondi Beach, people lie,
    like rows of fish laid out to dry,
    in the blazing sun.
They think it fun.
The sand is barely visible for pink bodies, sharing a vista
    denuded of trees,
Hordes of tourists from overseas, crowd
    iconic Bondi Beach.
They come from grey, wintry lands of snow.
Attracted like moths to a streetlight, they got to know the
    abandonment of stretching out beneath blazing sunlight
    that fades the sea like old denim,
        igniting spangles like broken bottles in the sands.
They soak up beer, chicks, and sparkle of sand and seas,
    before returning to dull jobs in grey cities,
    in far off lands.
Near Woy Woy, words evoking liquid echo of oars thrust deep
in water of a lagoon,
    I know a different beach.
A rim of verdant bush lies close, like a lover, to a beach of
golden sands.
A cacophonous band of birds jam in the bush,
    rhythms of a story nature is telling.
The bellbird's liquid call is belling,
    breaking the silence.
I feel grateful I was led here,
    to a different beach.

The Fortress

A bird is perched on a cliff face.
It soars down past black sluiced rock to roaring seas far below.
Waves gleam like fangs in the sea's dark maw.
When the tide is out, the bird feeds on shellfish,
    that dot the black rock face like stars.
A flock of birds wheel overhead,
    like a white cloud against the sky.
The birds come down, to feed, like drifts of snow on the cliff top.
Against the sky, in shadow, the cliff rises like an ancient fortress,
    now in ruins.
Birds, with sleek, oily feathers, and shrill cries, now dwell there,
feeding on fish far below.
The birds make nests, creating a home amidst scraps of withered grass.

Nature's Alchemy

Strange colours unfurled like banners in an alien green sky,
overhead, reflected in a glassy sea.
Clouds filled the harbour with reflections of jostling, orange
and purple clouds, struggling to escape the harbour confines.
The sea lay pale blue, like ice fields in the distance.
Darkness descended as the Manly ferry came in, dragging
reflections that were like a living entity; a pink iridescent
aqueous mass.
Reflections of buildings strobed the harbour with columns of
neon orange, red and green.
I suddenly thought of civilians in far off, diverse lands.
They look up to see the hatred, warfare and exploding missiles
of man,

    not nature's alchemy, overhead.

Pastel People

Hatred spills blood from hearth and home,
    through streets of crime,
    to battlefields of the world.
We pastel people on pastel shores,
    forget we all share the same hot, red blood
    that is spilled daily over planet earth.
The blue planet runs red with blood,
    while we fly like kites above the earth,
    flying on our beliefs,
    daring not to look down on the carnage

Memories of the Waikato, NZ

The first time the lady went to the Waikato,
    she saw tarns that glittered like diamonds,
    while white, fluffy clouds flew through the air.
She expected laughter and love to displace suspicion and fear.
Mists stalked the hills, denuded of tree cover,
    like ghosts of fallen Maori warriors,
    while young men demanded to be her lover.
Meanwhile the mighty Waikato River,
    lazy river, swollen and brown,
    sullen as it passes insolently through the town,
    snaking through tree cover,
    its reckless course gashing the earth.
Like a brown serpent, gorged and swollen,
    winding a sinuous course to the blue ocean.
The ocean remains always true to the sway of the moon,
    forever in love with Aotearoa, Land of the Long White Cloud,
    while the lady will return there never more.

Bad Attempts at Haiku

Rendezvous

By a course of least resistance,
Rivers flow to sea.
There is hope for me.

My Life Story

If my life were in print,
Would I live more fully?
Or just remain me.

Haiku not Ledgers

Taking the challenge,
I compose haiku,
Not balancing the ledgers.

Balance

Ignoring my work database,
To compose haiku,
I balance my soul.

Love

It must be LOVE;
He is stalking cockroaches again,
And then, he has replaced the fridge.

Six-line Stories

Write of Life

Writing keeps the life blood flowing.

My Brilliant Career

Work has more lurks than perks

Love Story

Loved and lost and alone again.

Requiem for a Friendship

Only their email address is left.

Meanwhile, On the Other Side of Town…

On the neat side of town,
    Benji, eyes gooey brown,
    wags his flamboyantly plumed tail
    at the postie delivering the mail.
When Benji feels dejected,
    sloppy kisses rejected,
    that magnificent tail gets droopy,
    falling like a horse's mane.
Benji's mistress got him from the pound.
What a tale his eyes could tell,
    how he was lost and never found,
    how upon hard times he fell.

While Benji wails, and wags his tail,
    'Elvis' has left the building,
    dragging rubbish bins.
He is yet another crooner who impersonates their 'king'.
In satin, sequins, diamonds, capes and things,
    he hopes to win 'Best Elvis' prize, that only one can win.

Meanwhile, on the other side of town…
The men are lean and mean and the dogs rough and tough,
    except for George, who as a watchdog sadly failed.
Leaving his post, George loudly wailed.
Like his Brit namesake, George is a true 'John Peel',
    preferring to squeal.
George refused to guard his master's guilty secrets it is said
    (perhaps a drug lab in the shed).

Further down lives a sturdy dyke, on a quest,
    saving money to build a love nest
    for her long-time girlfriend.
Doing long shifts without end,
    eyes underlined with black shadows,
    she looks sick and careworn,
    striving not to end up washed up and lovelorn.

Meanwhile, poor B— has drunk his way well past oblivion,
    on a course to meet an early death.
His mother had drawn her last breath,
    no time at all to raise her boy.
Her time had come and she had gone,
    long before he had broken his last toy.
His father too had passed away,
    leaving B— alone, one long sad day,
    to booze and snooze.

While G—, proclaimed by his wife as deaf demented,
    ignores how he is tormented.
Cunningly understanding, hearing, as he pleases,
    shuts out how his wife teases.
He decorates a garden strip with broken toys,
    long thrown away by little boys.
'A symptom of dementia,' says his wife, in scorn,
    at a creative spirit, newborn.

Elvis Has Left the Building

Elvis has left the building.
Can I believe my eyes?
Elvis has left the building;
He is dragging rubbish bins,
    of plastic, yellow, green and red,
    jet-black bob-cut square upon his head.
Among a thousand Elvises, gyrating pelvises,
    he is yet another 'king' among the 'kings',
    in satin, sequins, diamonds, capes and things.
They strut their stuff and sing,
    hoping to win the prize only one can win.
Crooning in a velvet voice, one year our Elvis won.

Sunset

A sunset unfurls like a banner
Above the Plaza;
Sublime meets the mundane.
Down by the inlet,
It is as if the sun has fallen in the water
Suffusing it with pink.
The leaves of gum trees are tipped with gold,
Writing a secret message across the sky.
Nearby, the silhouette of a roof carves a black triangle in a scarlet sky;
A mysterious pyramid as night falls,
The birds roost in trees,
And all the creatures of the night stir,
Winking golden eyes.

The Minotaur

The headmaster was stiff-backed,
Strutting in striped suit.
Fury was his nickname.
So many crazy people seemed to work in schools, back then,
Before I had discovered Zen.
'Another one for me!' he roared when a teacher took me past his den.
No one ever heard what happened, behind closed doors, to pupils who had erred.
Once, discovered seated in the wrong place,
I, along with desk and chair, came down on the other side of the room, transported by Fury,
Who lurked in dark labyrinthine corridors of my mind,
Like the mythic Minotaur, half-man half-beast.
My friend, Stephanie, could ride the wildest stallions, bareback,
Vaulting over them, if she chose,
On our way to school.
She was like the ancient bull dancers of Crete.
Lithe and slim,
They seized steers by the horns, leaping over them,
Landing square,
In the abundant age of Taurus the bull.
The dangerous dance symbolised outwitting the Minotaur, half-man half-bull,
Imagined in a labyrinth, deep within the Earth,
But really lurking within the soul of man.
Maybe we were both there, in ancient times,
She in the ring and I among the cheering throng.

Girl From Ithaca

I remember his name was Rainer.
He dressed me in a long dark magician's robe,
Embroidered in gold with suns and moons,
    'borrowed' from his father, the wily magician.

He told me I was a Grecian woman far from Ithaca,
My name, Adriana, almost an anagram of Rainer, means
'Dark-haired girl from the Adriatic Sea'.
In Ithaca I danced and sang;
Not like the serious present.

All that remained was his poem on a frail scrap of paper,
    Following me from one rented dwelling to the next,
    Until one day it was gone; vanished.

Like our love.

Strawberries

I don't buy strawberries any more.
They are sour, red on top,
Mushy brown further down.
Once I borrowed my brother's clothes,
When home on holiday,
To pick strawberries, paid by the punnet.
My mother wondered how I 'done it'.

Now there are vines in neat rows
To the horizon, with vineyard tours and dinner.
Boutique wines are a winner.

And I don't buy strawberries any more.

Poetry Versus Commerce

Poetry flows in a vacuum at the markets.
Each word rises,
Falling unheard.
Dedicated shoppers pass as if in a trance;
Mesmerised by bargains.
Word power is gutted by buying power.

Youth in their beauty

The long-legged boy, wavy hair to his shoulders,
Smiled jauntily and said 'Hello,'
Putting a bright face over his plight,
While to his right,
A young girl stood,
Round sweet face, hair tied back tight,
Ponytail hanging over her hood.
Like him, her smile was wide and bright,
T-shirt and denim-clad.
They laughed as if aggression made them glad,
To conceal they were really homeless and sad.
He had trashed their last place, sent away,
Now a sadder, sicker addict lets them stay.
They remind him of his lost youth,
While they rarely tell the truth,
Nor pay their way.
One day they leave, weaving slowly down the road,
Pushing a silver shopping trolley,
Clanging and bumping, carrying their load,
Resplendent in youth's beauty and folly.

A Puppy From the Skies

(based on a true story)

A hawk soars skyward,
A menacing black V.
A black squiggle dangles from his talons,
Shape shifting to a puppy.
Seized by the bird of prey
    From a greasy tip,
Where he'd been at play,
Slippery,
    Slithering,
        Free-falling,
            The puppy slides free.
A young girl catches him, hearing his cries,
Thanking God for her puppy from the skies.
The angry predator soars away
In search of easier prey.

Upon Gazing Into the Internet

Before Facebook, crystal globes were scried by see-ers of old,
Wise ones, to whom myriad mysteries would unfold.
An occult crystal ball might many secrets uncover,
Tales of knights, battles, and many a lady's secret lover.

Court gossip relayed such tales, not by silicon chips, and wires,
Nor by crystal globes, but twisted on the lips of devious liars.
In our modern age, rather than consulting a see-er, as of ancient days,
Those who would be wise must scree Internet ways.

Scandals and half-truths are broadcast through copper wire,
With sensationalised news, and gossip from many a liar.
The same old stories are still being told as half-truths, in place of fact,
With gossip and melodrama,
Devoid of truth and tact.

Elegy for the many lone deceased women not found until years after their death

Like spun silk was the lady's hair,
But no one held her dear.
From the north
They did not see her worth.
From the south,
They were just another greedy mouth.
From the east,
She was excluded from the lover's feast.
From the west
They were just like all the rest.
The tower was prepared,
The drawbridge down,
But the halls were empty,
With no lovers to crown.

In time her lonely tower became her tomb,
But no one called again.
The angels came then,
And reclaimed her soul,
Beyond human ken,
Removed from spite, beyond the night,
Released from the fear that had ruled her here,
Returned to the source of love.

Travels to my spare room

I jauntily took a trip, without him, on a whim,
To my spare room in the gloom,
Like a witch on a broom.
I gaze about me in wonder,
Discovering what my guests might see;
It's like a Holiday Inn without a key.
Movie posters awaken images
And I remember my life back then.
Shelves rich in treasured books,
Bring back the joy of when I first read them,
Sailing like an explorer on an inner journey.
A host of odds and ends, out of place elsewhere,
Now oddly fit together, like travelling companions, forgetting differences to share the journey.
Forgotten places bring back neglected spaces in me,
Inciting me to explore and break free.

Redundancy

The office windowpanes draw light as needy people pour
through the opened door,
Telling me of their plight.
Among them are those like spiritual ram-raiders in the night;
They know only how to smash and grab at the light.

Now government, office towers have fallen,
Leaving me alone, free.
But the power behind me is gone
And I seem an easy target for some;
Now I must face the murky light alone,
Only my intuition, like a trusted friend, to guide me.

For a friend

You don't look for every imagined flaw,
Nor pry or assume you know so much more.
We have shared lives in many diverse times and spaces;
Coming together and then moving far away.
Perhaps we met many lifetimes before,
On distant shores and places of this Earth,
Before rebirth.
To be a friend you don't have to live next door.

Susan

As a child, among my many dolls, in rows,
Susan, the newest doll, was dressed in yellow satin,
With skin of plastic sheen and rigid curls,
Glowing, in shiny shoes with bows.
Susan's plastic smile seemed treacherous,
Like a teacher, who with demure smile, tried to drown me once,
Plastic frozen expression, and mouth a livid red,
Like the walking dead,
With curls in ridges, as if painted on her head.
When in high school, there was a poem I read:
'The doll was called Christina,*
Her underwear was lace,
She smiled when you dressed her,
And then when you undressed her,
She kept a smiling face.
Until the day she tumbled,
And broke herself in two,
And her yellow head was hollow,
Behind her eyes of blue.'
The poet 'Went to bed with a lady
Somewhere seen before,
He heard the name Christina,
And suddenly saw Christina
Dead on the nursery floor.'
And I saw Susan, lying broken in a ditch.

* From the poem 'Christina' by Louis Macneice

High On Tea

I discover an ornate jar,
Deep in a cupboard, in the dark,
Filled with tea from many years ago,
Aromatic essences long distilled.
Memories come back of travels.
I remember imbibing the local tea, at dusk,
Brewed in a billy at twilight, over a fire,
With slices of Madeira cake steeped in sunshine;
Behind rolled the sylvan Daintree Forest.
A mountain rose, near perfect, like Mount Fuji,
Against a sunset steeping the sky with pink.

Essences of warm memories are distilled in the brew.
The jar is emptied of tea and memories.
Could it be that you and me
Spent an afternoon getting high on Daintree tea?

A Storyteller

I can hear the music of her words
In a story she is telling,
Like raindrops falling,
Evocative, trembling;
Drops of liquid gold held in a spider's web.
Her words are mesmerising,
Strung in a tantric pattern like beaded jewellery,
Or like a silken tapestry.

The light of my words

Mine is not a light that brightly shines
But dimly flickers and sputters,
Like a candle in the dark that never fully shines;
A lamp covered by a cloth.

My brain weaves words like a spider spinning silk.
I catch, in my net of words, only myself.

I was born with a multitude of words seeded in my soul from lifetimes spent before on this earth.
I must unravel the secret code, etched on my soul like tracks in the desert;
When the cache of words runs out my life will end.

Each hears only their own words above the steady drumbeat of their heart.
Yet the vibration of words moves our universe for us
While my world of words moves only for me.

Soulmate

I am the gentle breeze
That blows over your lake.
I am the oasis in your desert.
I am the cool breeze off the sea
I am the stream that quenches your thirst.
You are the fire that burns on my hearth,
And you shine like a torch in the darkness.

Another Fake

The beaded curtain tinkles in the breeze,
Reflecting harsh white light.
Red glass beads cast reflections on the polished floor,
Like crimson drops of blood.
The cards are fanned out.
The psychic crouches behind the curtain,
As if to see with her inner eye,
If she could, if she would.
The shop assistants seem to snigger,
As if at the fools who pass by the counter of trinkets.
The client anxiously wonders.
Will she hear,
Rape and obsession described as true love?
Helping the needy as her own bad luck?
Awareness of crime and street wisdom described as negativity?
Auric traces of previous customers,
And strife and dissension seen as her own aura?
She clings to the hope the psychic sees clearly,
And that her dilemma will be resolved,
Just as the psychic said it would,
While red beads cast jewel-shaped reflections on the polished floor,
Like Christ's blood.

Out Shopping

I walk alone weighed down by shopping.
A startled cat, in striped camouflage of fur,
Stops its headlong dash of fear,
As if dazzled by my silver shoes,
Caught in a sudden beam of light.
Meeting my gaze with dancing eyes, the cat appears to grin,
Sharing the fun,
That I too am a wanderer like him,
A creature that likes to dance on air,
On magic shoes from a flea mart.

Once home, I devour nectarines, crimson, with yellow flesh beneath the skin,
And amber juice drips down my chin.

No More Stories and Poems

They don't want poems and stories any more.
Marketing and merchandising
And advertising are the grinners.
Poems and stories now must come
Complete with bells and whistles,
Free offers,
And a markdown at the end of the day,
Before the sales.
Forget the writer.
Its all interactive now.
Just ring a call centre in India
And an overworked wage slave
Can write your poem in Hindi.
Pop-ups and advertising will appear,
Of cacophonous drums and dancing girls.

www.ingramcontent.com/pod-product-compliance
Lightning Source LLC
Chambersburg PA
CBHW062203100526
44589CB00014B/1934